AMAZING BRAIN GAMES for Clever Kids

Puzzles and solutions
by Dr Gareth Moore

B.Sc (Hons) M.Phil Ph.D

Illustrations and cover
artwork by Chris Dickason

Designed by Tall Tree Ltd

AMAZING BRAIN GAMES for Clever Kids

BUSTER BOOKS

First published in Great Britain in 2020 by Buster Books,
an imprint of Michael O'Mara Books Limited,
9 Lion Yard, Tremadoc Road, London SW4 7NQ

 www.mombooks.com/buster

 Buster Books

 @BusterBooks

 @buster_books

Clever Kids is a trade mark of Michael O'Mara Books Limited.

Puzzles and solutions © Gareth Moore 2020

Illustrations and layouts © Buster Books 2020

A CIP catalogue record for this book is available from the British Library.

ISBN: 978-1-78055-664-2

7 9 10 8 6

This product is made of material from well-managed, FSC®-certified
forests and other controlled sources. The manufacturing processes
conform to the environmental regulations of the country of origin.

Printed and bound in June 2024 by
CPI Group (UK) Ltd, Croydon, CR0 4YY.

MIX
Paper | Supporting
responsible forestry
FSC® C171272

INTRODUCTION

Get ready to push your brain to the limit and challenge your intellect in this fun-filled book!

Take your pick of over 100 brain-teasers, mind-benders and logic puzzles. You can complete the games in any order you like and work through at your own pace. Each puzzle gives you space to write down your answers and, when you're finished, you can check them against the solutions at the back.

Start each puzzle by reading the instructions. Sometimes this is the hardest part of the puzzle, so don't worry if you have to read the instructions a few times to be clear about what they mean. It's a good idea to write in pencil, so you can rub your answers out if they're not quite right (and then try again!).

INTRODUCTION

At the top of every page, there is a space for you to write how much time it took you to complete the puzzle on your first go. If you come back at a later date to try it again, you could then see if you've got faster at it.

If you really struggle with a puzzle, take a look at the solutions at the back to see how it works, then try it again later and see if you can do it in your head the second time round.

Good luck, and have fun!

Introducing the Brain Games Master:
Gareth Moore, B.Sc (Hons) M.Phil Ph.D

Dr Gareth Moore is an Ace Puzzler, and author of lots of puzzle books.

He created an online brain-training site called BrainedUp.com, and runs a puzzle site called PuzzleMix.com. Gareth has a Ph.D from the University of Cambridge, where he taught machines to understand spoken English.

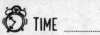
There's only one piece needed to complete this puzzle, but unfortunately some pieces from other jigsaws have been mixed in with the correct piece. Can you work out which piece should be used to complete the monster jigsaw?

Can you find all of the listed words in the grid? They can run in any direction, including diagonally.

All of the words are palindromes, which means that they remain exactly the same whether you read them forwards or backwards.

CIVIC	LEVEL	RADAR	SAGAS
DEIFIED	MADAM	REDDER	SEES
EYE	MINIM	REFER	SOLOS
KAYAK	NOON	ROTOR	WOW

K	I	N	C	I	V	I	C	I	R
D	A	R	O	T	O	R	R	E	O
R	W	Y	Y	O	E	E	D	V	O
D	A	M	A	Y	N	D	S	O	R
E	S	A	E	K	E	L	S	R	E
I	A	D	D	R	E	O	A	M	F
F	G	A	E	V	L	D	I	W	E
I	A	M	E	O	A	N	E	O	R
E	S	L	S	R	I	A	K	W	E
D	I	Y	D	M	S	E	E	S	C

Draw horizontal and vertical lines to join all of the circles into pairs, so that each pair consists of one white and one shaded circle.

The lines you draw to join the circles cannot cross each other. They also can't cross over other circles.

Take a look at the example solution to see how this works:

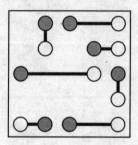

a)

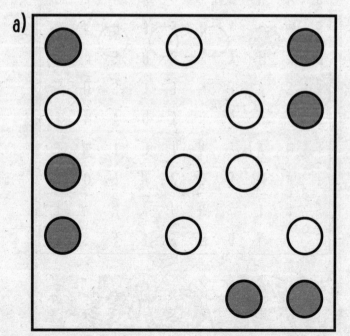

For each of the following puzzles, can you see which of the four options (a to d) is most likely to replace the question mark in order to complete the sequence of four images?

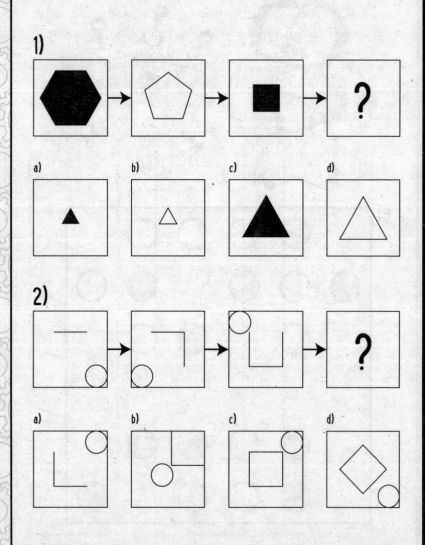

1)

a)   b)   c)   d)

2)

a)   b)   c)   d)

Can you solve these brain chains in your head, without writing down any numbers until the final answer?

Start with the value at the top of each puzzle, then follow each arrow in turn and do what the mathematical instructions say until you reach the 'RESULT' box. Write the final value you have in that box.

For example, in the first puzzle you would start with 13, then add 9, then divide by 2, and so on until you reach the bottom.

a)

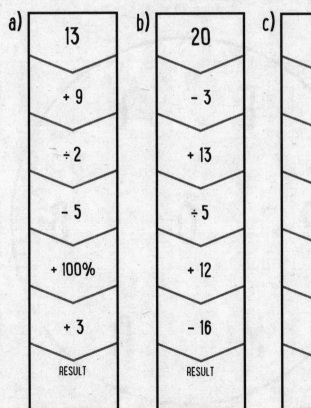

13
+ 9
÷ 2
− 5
+ 100%
+ 3
RESULT
....

b)

20
− 3
+ 13
÷ 5
+ 12
− 16
RESULT
....

c)

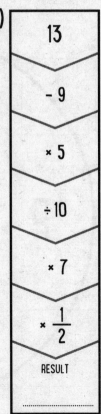

13
− 9
× 5
÷ 10
× 7
× $\frac{1}{2}$
RESULT
....

How many words can you find in this word circle? Each word should use the central letter plus two or more of the other letters. You can't use a letter more than once in a word. There is also one word that uses all seven of the letters.

TARGETS:

Good: **8 words**

Excellent: **14 words**

Amazing: **20 words**

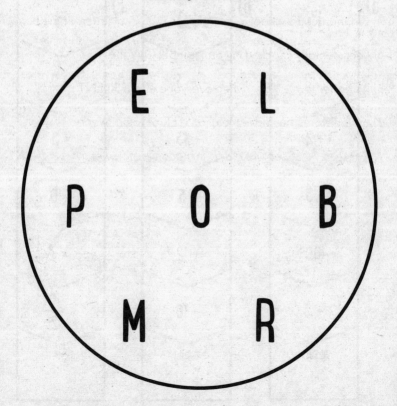

Can you fill in the missing word in each of the following anagram sentences? Each word must use the same letters as the word written in capitals, but in a different order.

The first one is done for you, as an example.

1) I am proud to OWN lots of trophies that I have WON .

2) We keep the largest cooking .... on the TOP shelf.

3) The LAST thing to add to the recipe is some ....

4) On the way to school, I .... to POST my letters in the box.

5) I accidentally knocked my arm just BELOW the ....

6) It's easier to .... when everyone else is SILENT.

7) At the store, they gave me a TASTER of some sweet ....

8) These PLATES feature a design made up of flower ....

Two of these green-fingered monsters are identical, except for their rotation, but the third is slightly different to the rest. Which monster picture is the odd one out?

For each of these two puzzles, can you draw a loop that visits every white square? The loop can only travel horizontally or vertically between touching squares, and cannot enter any square more than once.

This example solution should help show you how it works:

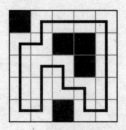

a)

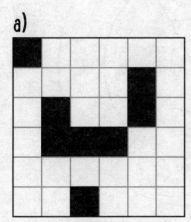

b)

Can you form each of the given sums by choosing one number from each ring of this dartboard and then adding them all together?

For example, you could form a sum of 10 by picking 1 from the innermost ring, 2 from the middle ring and 7 from the outermost ring.

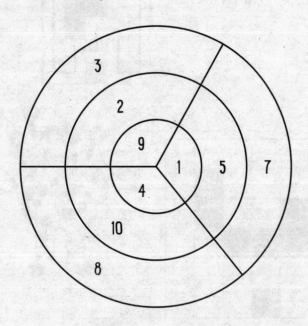

TARGET SUMS:

11 = ...
16 = ...
26 = ...

This picture has been created purely by drawing various circles. How many separate circles were used?

Total: ....

Can you solve each of these sudoku puzzles?

All you need to do is place a number from 1 to 4 into every empty square. You must do this in such a way that no number repeats in any row, column or bold-lined 2x2 box.

Take a look at this example solution to see how the puzzle works:

2	1	4	3
3	4	1	2
4	2	3	1
1	3	2	4

a)

	4	2	
2	3	1	4
4	1	3	2
	2	4	

b)

1			2
	3	4	
	1	2	
3			4

c)

		3	
1			
			4
	2		

How many words can you find by travelling inwards from the outside ring to the centre ring, picking one letter from each ring in turn? For example, you could pick 'R', 'U' and 'N' to spell 'RUN'.

Can you find 10 different words?

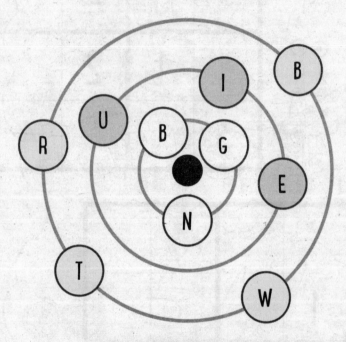

For an extra challenge, can you find 5 further words?

There are six differences between these two pictures of this monster inventor. Can you find them all?

Can you draw a series of separate paths to connect each pair of identical monster symbols together?

The paths must not cross or touch each other, and no more than one path can enter any grid square. Each path must be made up of only horizontal and vertical lines. No diagonal lines are allowed.

Take a look at this example solution to see how it works, and then try the three following puzzles:

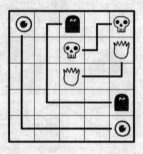

a)

b)

c)

⏰ TIME ....

Can you draw three straight lines to divide the area below into four separate regions, so that each region contains exactly one of each type of monster?

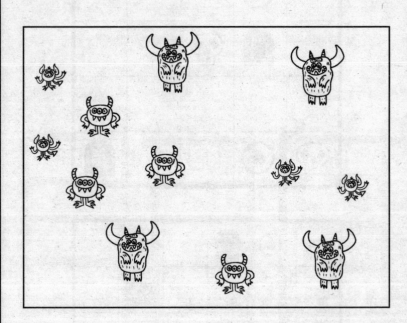

Can you complete each of these word ladders? The aim is to climb down from the top word to the bottom word in a fixed number of steps. Each step must contain an English word, and that word must be the same as the word below it but with just one letter changed — and none of the letters can be arranged into a different order.

For example, you could move from CAT to DOG like this:

CAT ➡ COT ➡ DOT ➡ DOG

Can you fill in each of these number pyramids? Each block should contain a number equal to the sum of the two blocks immediately beneath it.

Take a look at this example solution to see how it works, and then try the three following puzzles:

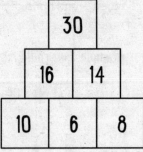

30

16 | 14

10 | 6 | 8

a)

11 | 10 | 10

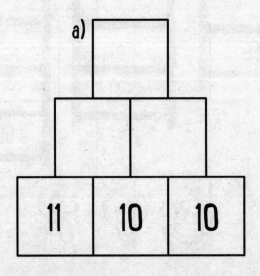

b)

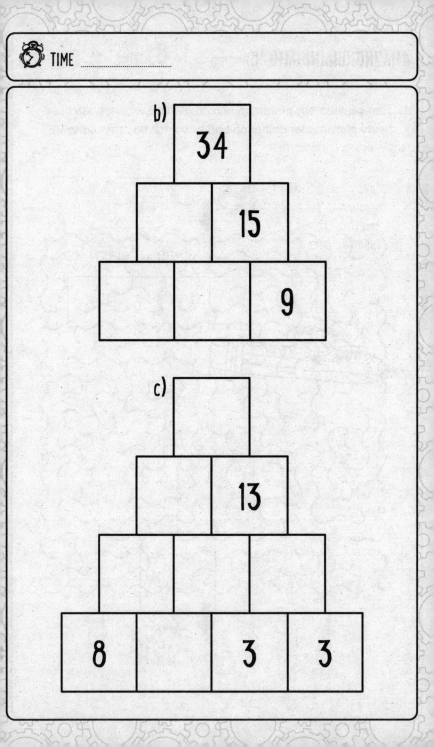

	34	

		15	

		9

c)

	13	

| 8 | | 3 | 3 |

Can you help this monster find a path all the way through this twisty maze? Enter at the top and exit at the bottom, as shown.

Take a look at the monsters below and spend a minute or two remembering what they look like. Then, when you're ready, turn to the next page where three new monsters will have joined the group. Can you circle all of the new monsters?

Circle the new monsters:

Complete the grid so each number from 1 to 16 appears once, and so that you can trace a path from 1 through to 16 simply by following the arrows from square to square. Arrows point at the next square in the sequence, which does not have to be touching.

In this example solution, notice how the 1 points at the 2, which then points at the 3, which points to the 4, and so on through to 16:

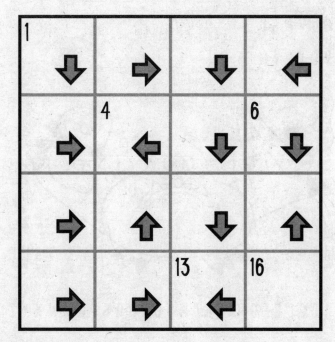

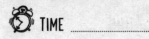 ⏱ TIME ....

Can you work out what the following six coded words have in common?

To crack the code, replace each letter with the letter that would be in the same position if the alphabet was reversed. This means, for example, that you should replace A with Z, B with Y, and so on all the way through to replacing Z with A.

1) G D L ....

2) H V E V M ....

3) M R M V ....

4) G D V O E V ....

5) G D V M G B ....

6) V O V E V M ....

A B C D E F G H I J K L M N O P Q R S T U V W X Y Z

Can you find the seven dominoes that complete this circuit? Place one of the ten loose dominoes on to each shaded domino in order to complete the loop, but without using any of the dominoes more than once. Dominoes can only touch one another if they have the same number of spots on the touching ends.

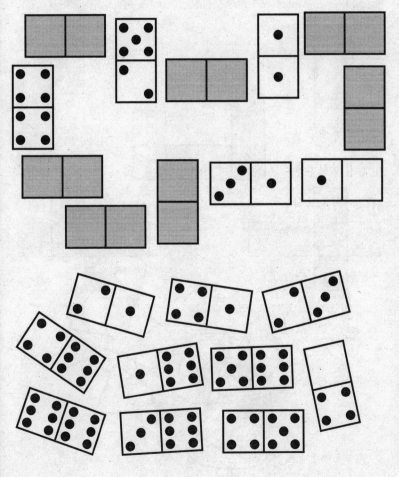

Four of these five shapes could be cut out and then folded along the lines to form complete six-sided cubes. One of them could not, however. Which is the odd one out?

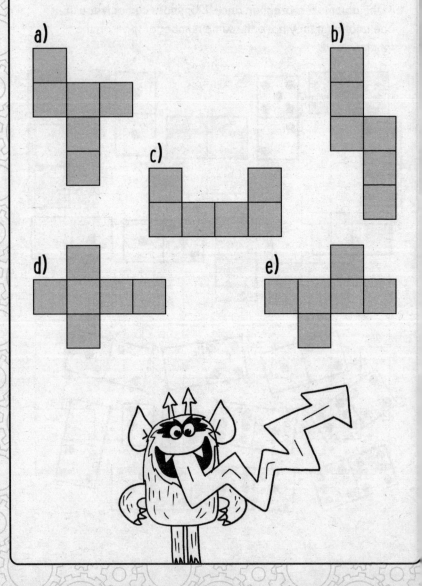

a)

b)

c)

d)

e)

Solve this maze by finding a route from the entrance at the top of the maze to the exit at the bottom. Then, add up all of the numbers on the direct route from the entrance to the exit, ignoring any dead ends you previously travelled along. What is the total of all of those values?

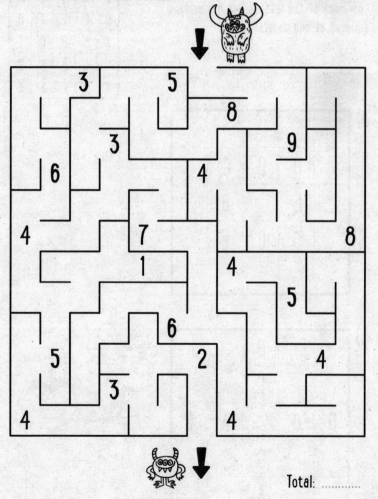

Total: ....

Can you place a letter from A to E into every empty square, so that no letter repeats in any row or column? Identical letters can't be in touching squares — not even diagonally.

Take a look at this example solution and notice how none of the letters are in touching squares at any point:

E	A	B	D	C
D	C	E	A	B
A	B	D	C	E
C	E	A	B	D
B	D	C	E	A

a)

	B	D	C	
	E		B	
	D	C	E	

b)

		B		
		E		
D	B		A	E
		D		
		A		

This monster loves healthy food. Can you help him find all of the items listed below in the grid? They can be written either forwards or backwards and can run in any direction, including diagonally.

BEANS	GARLIC	OATS	VEGETABLES
CHEESE	LEAN MEAT	OLIVE OIL	WATER
EGGS	LENTILS	PULSES	YOGHURT
FISH	LETTUCE	RICE	
FRUIT	NUTS	SEEDS	

F	S	O	S	T	R	U	H	G	O	Y	C
R	T	V	L	B	F	S	S	L	T	L	H
U	R	E	A	I	E	G	E	T	G	S	E
I	L	G	V	R	A	S	S	A	E	E	E
T	E	E	S	R	E	E	N	E	L	O	S
E	N	T	E	T	C	T	O	S	G	U	E
I	T	A	S	C	S	I	A	I	E	G	P
E	I	B	F	N	U	E	L	W	L	B	S
C	L	L	I	U	I	T	E	R	S	E	L
I	S	E	S	T	S	A	T	D	A	S	I
R	L	S	H	S	A	U	S	E	S	G	G
E	L	E	A	N	M	E	A	T	L	G	E

Take a look at these monsters. How quickly can you count the following:

a) How many eyes can you count in total? ....

b) How many monsters are showing their teeth or their tongue? ....

c) How many are looking towards the left-hand side of the page? ....

d) How many monsters have exactly five limbs? ....
(A limb is a leg, arm or tentacle, so count the total number of legs, arms and tentacles on each monster. Don't include wings or tails in your count.)

e) How many have six limbs?

f) If you add together the number of limbs, eyes and teeth on each monster, how many have a total of ten or more? ....

Can you identify each of the following numerical sequences, then work out which number should come next? For example, if the sequence was 15, 17, 19, 21, 23 then the sequence would be 'add 2 at each step', so the next number would be 25.

a)   6   13   20   27   34   41   ....

The sequence is ....

b)   115   103   91   79   67   55   ....

The sequence is ....

c)   256   128   64   32   16   8   ....

The sequence is ....

d)   123   234   345   456   567   678   ....

The sequence is ....

e) $\frac{1}{3}$ 1   3   9   27   81   ....

The sequence is ....

The following nine tiles can be cut out and rearranged to form a picture of a black capital letter. Can you work out which one? You don't need to rotate any of the tiles, and they will form a 3x3 grid.

Hint: If you're struggling to find the answer, try working through each letter of the alphabet in turn, from A to Z, until you find the answer. For each letter, see if you have all the parts you would need to make that capital letter.

Can you fill in the empty squares so that each grid contains every number from 1 to 16 once each. There is just one rule, which is that you must be able to start at '1' and then move to '2', '3', '4' and so on by moving only to touching grid squares. You can only move left, right, up and down between squares, and not diagonally.

Take a look at this example solution to see how it works:

10	9	8	1
11	12	7	2
16	13	6	3
15	14	5	4

a)

4			7
	10	9	
	11	14	
1			16

b)

1			16
4			13

How many words of three or more letters can you find hidden in this grid? Start on any letter and then trace a path to touching letters, including diagonally touching letters, to spell out a word. You can't use a letter square more than once in any word. For example, you could start on 'T', move to 'R' and then to 'Y' to spell 'TRY'.

There is one word that uses all of the letters.

TARGETS:

Good: 8 words

Excellent: 12 words

Amazing: 16 words

M	S	T
Y	R	E
I	E	S

This monster has a bunch of balloons, each of which has a different number painted on it:

Which balloons would you burst so that the numbers on those remaining add together to form each of the following totals? For example, you could form a total of 7 by bursting all except the 4 and 3 balloons, since 4 + 3 = 7.

Which balloons would you burst to reach the following totals?

a) 10 ....

b) 16 ....

c) 26 ....

Can you join all of the dots to form a single loop that visits every dot?

You can only use straight horizontal or vertical lines to join dots, and the loop can't cross or touch itself.

Some parts of the loop have already been drawn in to get you started.

Take a look at this example solution to see how it works:

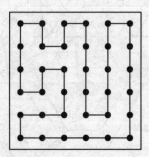

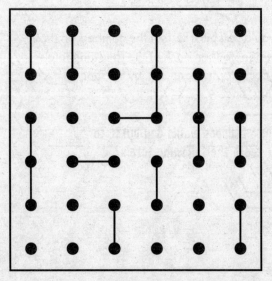

Can you help this monster find a path all the way through this angular maze? Enter at the top and exit at the bottom, as shown.

How many building-block cubes have been used to create the picture at the bottom of this page? None of the cubes are floating in mid-air.

The picture started off as this 4x4x3 arrangement of 48 cubes, as shown, before some were removed:

 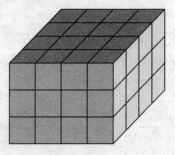

How many cubes are in this picture?

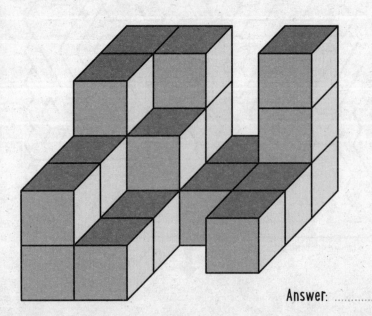

Answer: ....

It's quiz time! See how many of the following multiple-choice questions you can answer.

1) Which two of these paints will make purple when they are mixed together?

        a) Green and blue   b) Red and blue
        c) Red and orange   d) Yellow and blue

2) Which of the following animal's babies are called 'cygnets'?

        a) Salmon   b) Seal
        c) Sheep   d) Swan

3) Which author wrote *Charlie and the Chocolate Factory* and *Matilda*?

        a) A. A. Milne   b) C. S. Lewis
        c) Jacqueline Wilson   d) Roald Dahl

4) For which of the following was Florence Nightingale most famous?

        a) As a cyclist   b) As a gardener
        c) As a nurse   d) As a musician

5) What is Diwali the Hindu festival of?

        a) Elephants   b) Lights
        c) Music   d) Summer

Can you solve these two Futoshiki puzzles by placing the numbers 1 to 4 once each into every row and column?

You must obey the arrows, which act as 'greater than' and 'less than' signs. The arrows always point from the bigger number to the smaller number of a pair. This means that, for example, you could have '2 > 1' since 2 is greater than 1, but '1 > 2' would be wrong because 1 is not greater in value than 2.

Take a look at this example to see how it works:

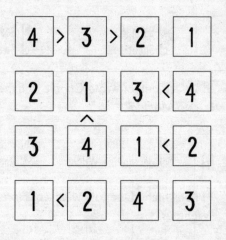

a)

4			2
∨			
	<		
∨			∨
	4	2 <	
∧			
3		>	1

b)

			3
		∧	∧
		2	
	∧		
	4	>	
		∧	∨
2			

Can you place all of the listed words into the grid? Each word can be written either horizontally or vertically, and each word is used exactly once each. They are sorted by length to help you work out which words can fit in which gaps.

HINT: Start by thinking about which word can fit in the first column. Only one of the two options will let you connect other words to it.

3 LETTERS
Awe
Hum
Lip
Sea
Set
Sum

4 LETTERS
Core
Lens
Scan
Trio

6 LETTERS
Castle
Engine
Gateau
Throne

7 LETTERS
Athlete
Cottage
Emperor
Glitter
Present
Student

11 LETTERS
Arrangement
Politicians

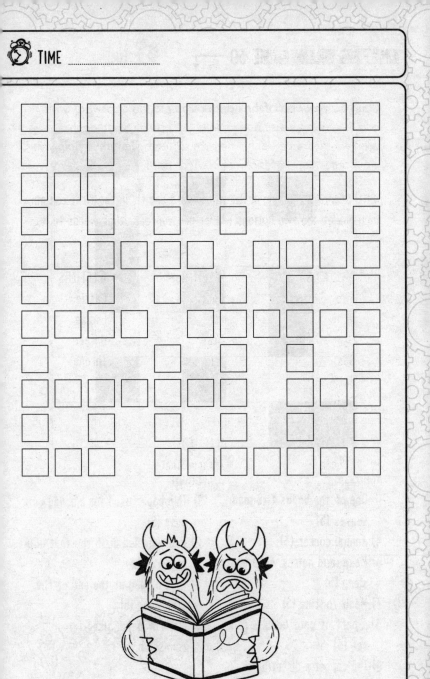

Can you answer all the clues to complete this crossword grid?

ACROSS
1) One of the body's five main senses (5)
4) Animal doctor (3)
6) Make loud noises while you sleep (5)
7) Magic routine (5)
8) A part of your body used to see (3)
9) The opposite direction to left (5)

DOWN
1) Thin paper used for blowing your nose (6)
2) Two-wheeled push toy that you stand on (7)
3) Time of day at the end of the afternoon (5)
5) Piece of paper used for admission (6)

Can you use your powers of deduction to work out which of the grid squares contain hidden mines in each of these two puzzles?

- Any empty grid square can contain a mine, but none of the numbered squares do.

- A number in a square tells you how many mines there are in touching squares, including diagonally touching squares.

Take a look at this example solution to see how it works:

	1	0
💀		1
💀	3	💀

a)

2		1
	3	
1		

b)

		1
	4	2
1		

⏱ TIME ....

These pictures all look similar, but there are in fact three identical pairs. Can you join the monsters into their matching-image pairs?

Can you build a word pyramid by solving each of the clues, one per row? When solved, each row should contain the same set of letters as the row above plus one extra letter. The letters can be rearranged into a different order.

For example, you might have DOG on the top row, then add an 'L' and rearrange the letters to make GOLD. Next, you might add an 'E' and rearrange again to make LODGE, and so on until the pyramid is filled.

Clues:

1) You listen with this

2) If you are very cautious, then you are taking this.

3) Very tall machine used for lifting things

4) Sugary fluid collected by bees from flowers

5) Absolutely sure of something

6) Woodwind instrument with a reed mouthpiece

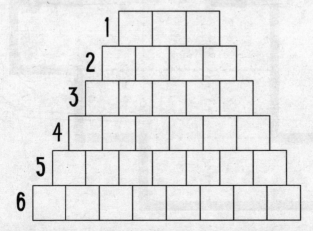

Can you draw along some of the dashed lines to divide this shape up into four identical pieces, with no unused parts left over?

Each of the four pieces must be identical, although they can be rotated relative to one another.

Take a look at this example solution to see how it works:

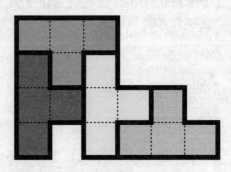

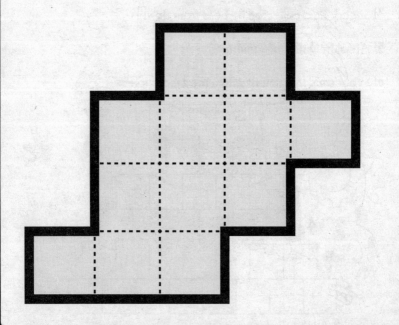

 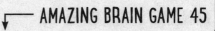

Amy, Bud and Cat all have their monster birthdays today. By reading the following clues, can you work out which birthday each monster is celebrating?

- Bud is neither the oldest nor the youngest of the three.

- Two years ago, Cat was twice the age that Amy was.

- The sum of Bud and Cat's ages is equal to three times Amy's age.

- All of the monsters are younger than ten years old.

Amy is ....   Bud is ....   Cat is ....

Draw horizontal and vertical lines to join all of the circles into pairs, so that each pair consists of one white and one shaded circle.

The lines you draw to join circles cannot cross over other lines, or over any circle.

Take a look at this example solution to see how it works:

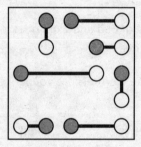

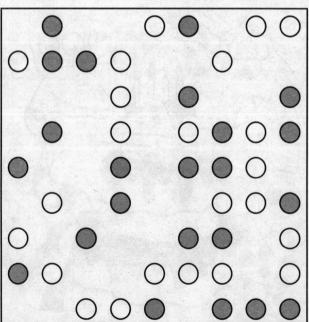

Study the objects below and spend a minute or two remembering what they look like. Then, when you're ready, turn to the next page where three of the objects will have vanished. Can you write down the names of those missing objects?

For example, if you think the teapot has vanished, write down 'teapot'.

⏰ TIME ....

Which three objects have vanished?

The missing items are:

....

....

....

Can you solve these brain chains in your head, without writing down any numbers until the final answer?

Start with the value at the top of each puzzle, then follow each arrow in turn and do what the mathematical instructions say until you reach the 'RESULT' box. Write the final value you have in that box.

For example, in the first puzzle you would start with 17, then add 13, then subtract 1, and so on until you reach the bottom.

a)

17
+ 13
– 1
+ 4
÷ 3
+ 100%
RESULT
....

b)

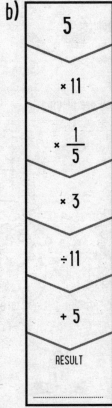

5
× 11
× $\frac{1}{5}$
× 3
÷ 11
+ 5
RESULT
....

c)

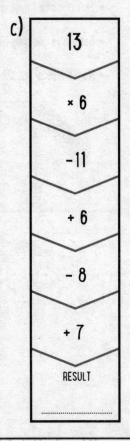

13
× 6
– 11
+ 6
– 8
+ 7
RESULT
....

Heather, Nadia and Bobbie all have parts in their school production of *A Midsummer Night's Dream*. Their characters are Helena, Hermia and Hippolyta. They are all going to wear different hats for the performance, where one hat is purple, one is orange and one is green.

By reading the following clues, can you complete the empty table to show who is playing which part, and wearing which hat?

- The person playing Hermia has a green hat.

- Bobbie is playing Hippolyta.

- Nadia has a purple hat.

Person	Part they are playing	Hat they are wearing

Can you say which of the four options (a to d) is most likely to replace the question mark in order to complete the sequences of four images?

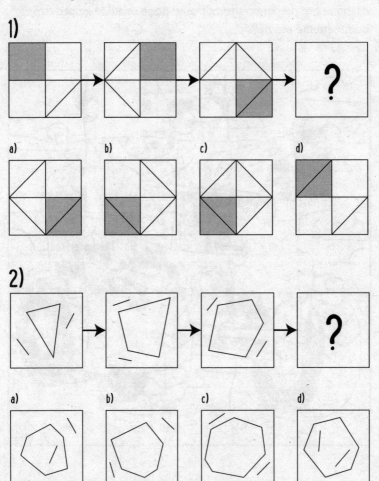

1)

a) b) c) d)

2)

a) b) c) d)

There are three pieces needed to complete this monster truck puzzle, but unfortunately some pieces from other jigsaws have been mixed in with the correct pieces. Can you work out which of the seven pieces on the opposite page should be used to complete the puzzle?

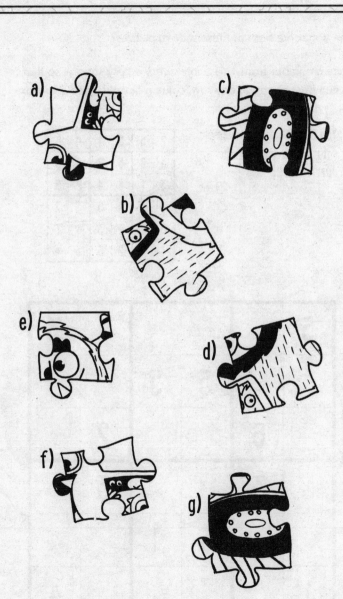

Can you solve both of these sudoku puzzles?

Place a number from 1 to 6 into every empty square, so that no number repeats in any row, column or bold-lined 2x3 box.

You can check this example solution to see how the puzzle works:

2	5	3	1	4	6
4	6	5	2	1	3
3	1	6	4	2	5
6	4	1	5	3	2
5	2	4	3	6	1
1	3	2	6	5	4

a)

5					3
		3	5		
	6			2	
	3			5	
		5	1		
1					4

b)

5					3
	2			1	
		6	5		
		3	2		
	5			4	
2					6

In the far-off land of Coinrobia, there are six different values of coin:

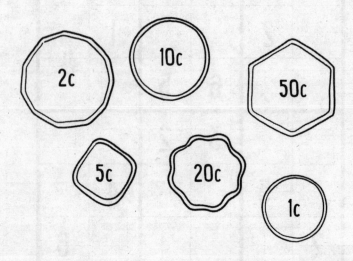

See if you can answer the following questions about these coins:

1) If you paid with five 10c coins, how much change would you be owed if you bought something that cost 43c?

2) You have exactly 85c in your pocket. What is the fewest number of coins that this could be made up of?

3) What is the most expensive item you could buy without using the same value of coin more than once?

4) What is the greatest number of coins I could use to pay for something costing 50c, if I wanted to use exact change and not use the same value of coin more than twice?

Five of these six shapes could be cut out and then folded along the lines to form complete six-sided cubes. One of them could not, however. Which is the odd one out?

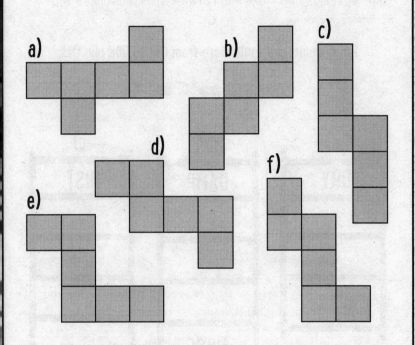

Can you complete each of these word ladders? The aim is to climb down from the top word to the bottom word in a fixed number of steps. Each step must contain an English word, and that word must be the same as the word below it but with just one letter changed — and none of the letters rearranged into a different order.

For example, you could move from CAT to DOG like this:

CAT ➡ COT ➡ DOT ➡ DOG

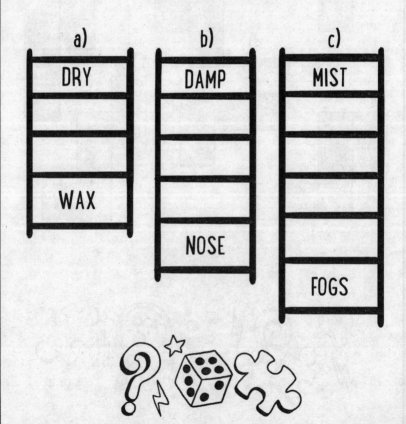

a)

DRY

WAX

b)

DAMP

NOSE

c)

MIST

FOGS

Can you fill in the missing word in each of the following anagram sentences? Each word must use the same letters as the word written in capitals, but in a different order.

The first one is done for you, as an example.

1) I rubbed some GEL on my sore LEG .

2) The OWL flew very .... over the field.

3) Sometimes I feel WEAK when I first .... up.

4) The magician found her .... at DAWN.

5) I managed to catch and SAVE the .... when it fell over.

6) In the dim light, the .... on the ring looked PALER.

7) The .... superhero PACED around the room.

8) When the ground QUAKES, I hear my pet mouse ....

Can you place all of the listed words into the grid? Each word can be written either horizontally or vertically, and each word is used exactly once each. They are sorted by length to help you work out which words can fit in which gaps.

3 LETTERS
Pod
Ton

4 LETTERS
Book
Cola
Easy
Shoe

5 LETTERS
After
Disco
Stand
Video

6 LETTERS
Gloves
Parrot
Robber
Safari

7 LETTERS
Blossom
Teacher

9 LETTERS
Adventure
Everybody
Impatient
Spaghetti

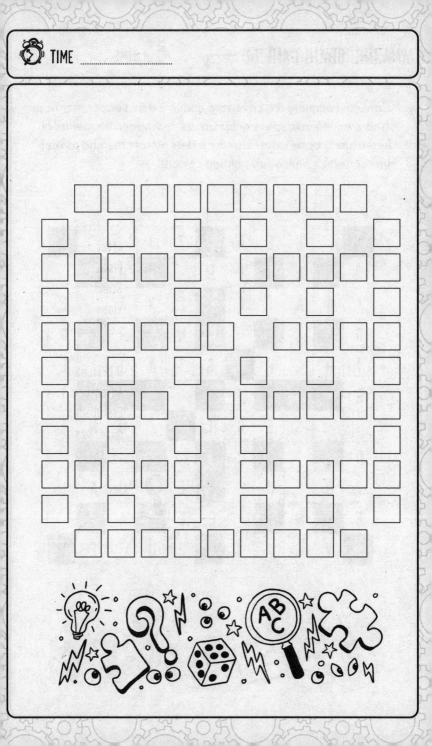

Can you complete this crossword grid by adding each letter from A to Z once each, so every horizontal and vertical sequence of letters spells out a word? Use the letters outside the grid to keep track of which ones you've already placed.

Can you help this monster find a path all the way through this circular maze? Enter at the top and exit at the bottom, as shown.

Can you form each of the given sums by choosing one number from each ring of this dartboard and then adding them all together?

For example, you could form a sum of 10 by picking 2 from the innermost ring, 5 from the middle ring and 3 from the outermost ring.

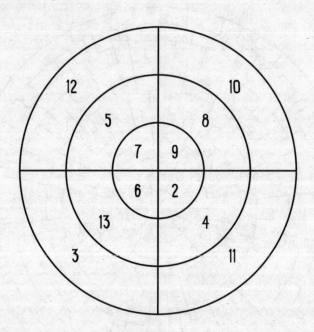

TARGET SUMS:

19 = ...
28 = ...
33 = ...

Each of these two pictures shows the same background image, but in each case different parts of it are covered by white squares.

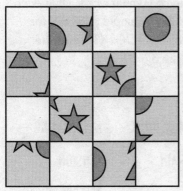 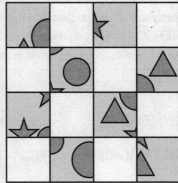

By imagining combining the two pictures, so the white squares on one are replaced with the corresponding squares from the other picture, answer the following questions:

a) How many stars are there?

b) How many circles are there?

c) How many triangles are there?

Can you find all of the listed words and phrases in the grid? They can be written either forwards or backwards, and can run in any direction including diagonally.

To find them, you'll need to replace a number word within each entry with its corresponding digits. For example to search for 'TO GO NEXT' you'd need to look for 'TOG1XT', since the 'ONE' needs to be replaced with the digit '1'.

ABANDONED	THREE-DIMENSIONAL	NETWORKING
ANCIENT WORLD	FREIGHT TRAIN	TENSION
ARTWORK	HEIGHTS	TELEPHONE
ATTENDANT	HIGH FIVE	THE FOUR WINDS
BREAKS EVEN	INTENTION	THORNINESS
CANINE TOOTH	MONEY BOX	WEIGHTLIFTING

```
H 3 N F R 8 T R A I N E P
T 8 D L R 2 N E I C N A A
H H S I B A N M 1 Y B O X
E 2 T N M B R E A K 7 1 I
4 I 4 O E E M 2 W 5 T H T
W N G N O D N 8 R N G P H
I O L N T T L S A K D E O
N I N 2 I I 9 D I S 1 L R
D T E O F K 0 A 5 O D E 9
S 0 G T I I R H C Y N T S
S 1 I I T S G 2 N 2 A A S
A N W A T I 0 G E H B I L
G I H R H 8 B 1 N N A N O
```

How many words can you find in this word circle? Each word should use the central letter plus two or more of the other letters. You can't use a letter more than once in a word. There are also two words that use all seven of the letters, although one of them is much easier to find than the other.

TARGETS:

Good: 15 words

Excellent: 25 words

Amazing: 35 words

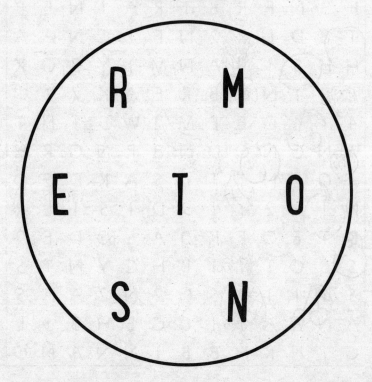

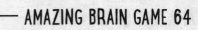

Take a look at these various fruits. How quickly can you count how many:

1) Are bananas? ....

2) Have a stalk with leaves hanging from the stalk? ....

3) Have had a bite taken out of them? ....

4) Have a worm coming out of them? ....

5) Are either an apple or pear and have no stalk? ....

Can you complete this grid so that every row, column and bold-lined region contains each of the letters from A to E once each?

Take a look at this example solution to see how the puzzle works:

D	C	B	E	A
A	E	D	B	C
C	B	E	A	D
B	A	C	D	E
E	D	A	C	B

a)

E				
			D	
	B		E	
	C			
				B

b)

				D
			B	
	E			
A				

Complete the grid so each number from 1 to 16 appears once, and so that you can trace a path from 1 through to 16 simply by following the arrows from square to square. Arrows point at the next square in the sequence, which does not have to be touching.

In this example solution, notice how the 1 points at the 2, which then points at the 3, which points to the 4, and so on through to 16:

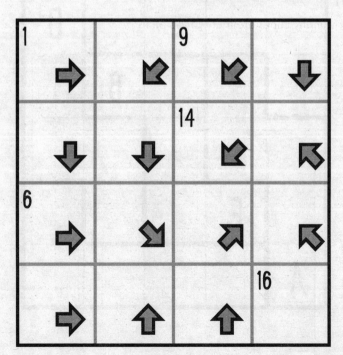

How many building-block cubes have been used to create the picture at the bottom of this page? The picture started off as this 4x4x4 arrangement of 64 cubes, as shown, before some were removed:

How many cubes are there in this picture?

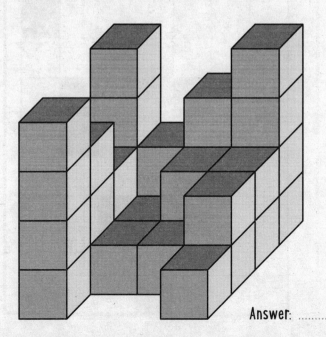

Answer: ....

Can you solve this puzzle by drawing a loop that visits every white square? The loop can only travel horizontally or vertically between touching squares, and cannot enter any square more than once.

This example solution should help show you how it works:

Can you fill in both of these number pyramids? Each block should contain a number equal to the sum of the two blocks immediately beneath it.

Take a look at this example solution to see how it works:

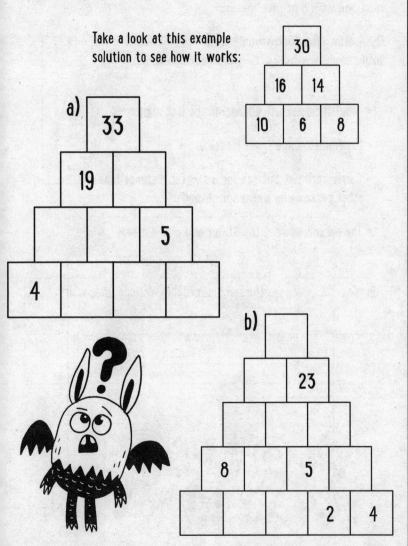

It's sports day, and Mohammed, Tallulah and Carrie have all won medals in different events: the 100m sprint, 400m sprint and the long jump. Also, one won a gold medal, one won a silver medal and one won a bronze medal.

By reading the following clues, can you complete the empty table to show who won which medal, in which race?

- Tallulah did not win a medal in the long jump.

- Mohammed won a silver medal.

- Carrie sprinted, but ran for a shorter distance than the other person who won a sprint medal.

- The person who ran the 400m won a gold medal.

Person	Race they won a medal in	Medal they won

Can you build a word pyramid by solving each of the clues, one per row? When solved, each row should contain the same set of letters as the row above plus one extra letter. The letters can be rearranged into a different order.

For example, you might have DOG on the top row, then add an 'L' and rearrange the letters to make GOLD. Next, you might add an 'E' and rearrange again to make LODGE, and so on until the pyramid is filled.

Clues:

1) Pose someone a question

2) Something to be done, such as an errand

3) A stick with a pointed end

4) The part of a hot-air balloon you can ride in

5) A disappointment which makes it harder to complete something

6) These punctuation symbols: (and)

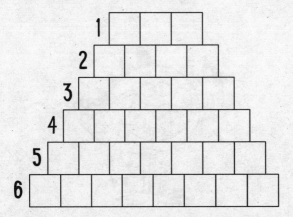

Can you answer all the clues to complete this crossword grid?

ACROSS

1) Event where something unfortunate happens by chance (8)

5) Fasten, as in '........... your shoelaces' (3)

6) Red liquid flowing around your body (5)

8) Large tropical fruit with tough, spiky skin (9)

10) Follow someone's movements (5)

13) The entire quantity of something (3)

15) Cupboard for hanging clothes (5)

DOWN

1) Drawings, painting, sculptures and music (3)

2) Tidy up; neaten (5)

3) Type of fish that looks a bit like a snake (3)

4) An even number just less than three (3)

6) Opposite of white (5)

7) Expected to arrive (3)

8) Deep, round container (3)

9) Keyboard instrument (5)

11) How meat is before it is cooked (3)

12) Common road vehicle (3)

14) Tell a fib (3)

1		2			3		4	■
_	■	_	■■■	_	■	_	■
5		_	■	6				7
■■	_	■	_	■			_
8						9		
_	■■■	_	■	_	■■■	_
10	11		12		13		14
■	_	■	_	■■	_	■	_
■	15						

Four of these monsters are identical, except for their rotation, but the fifth is slightly different to the rest. Which monster is the odd one out?

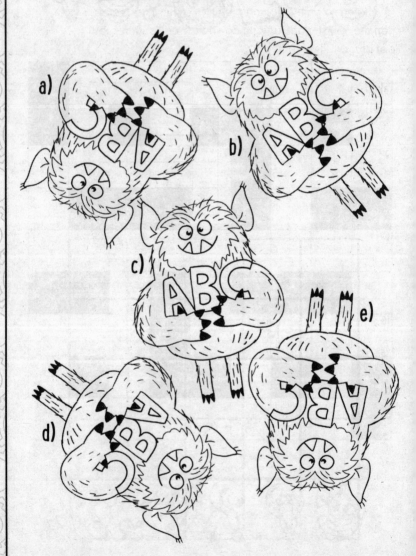

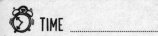
Can you fill in the empty squares so that each grid contains every number from 1 to 25 once each? There is just one rule, which is that you must be able to start at '1' and then move to '2', '3', '4' and so on by moving only to touching grid squares. You can move left, right, up and down between squares, but not diagonally.

Take a look at this example solution to see how it works:

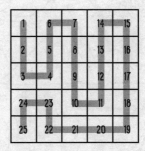

		13		
	15		3	
23		1		9
	17		5	
		19		

There are fifteen differences between these two scenes from the Monster Olympics. Can you find them all?

Can you draw a series of separate paths to connect each pair of identical monster symbols together?

The paths must not cross or touch each other, and no more than one path can enter any grid square. Each path must be made up of only horizontal and vertical lines. No diagonal lines are allowed.

Take a look at this example solution to see how it works, and then try both of the puzzles on the opposite page:

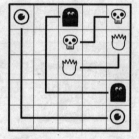

a)

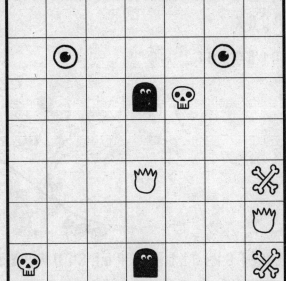

b)

Can you work out what the following six coded words have in common?

To crack the code, replace each letter with a letter in the alphabet. All the letters within each word use the same code, so either all the letters within a word are one place forward or one place back.

1) **MJNF**   ....

2) **LDKNM**   ....

3) **BQQMF**   ....

4) **HSBQF**   ....

5) **BGDQQX**   ....

6) **QJOFBQQMF**   ....

ABCDEFGHIJKLMNOPQRSTUVWXYZ

By tracing along the lines, how many separate rectangles can you count in this image? For example, there is one formed by the border all around the image.

This monster has a bunch of balloons, each of which has a different number painted on it.

Which balloons would you burst so that the numbers on those remaining add together to form each of the following totals? For example, you could form a total of 9 by bursting all except the 4 and 5 balloons, since 4 + 5 = 9.

Which balloons would you burst to reach the following totals?

a) 15 ....

b) 18 ....

c) 23 ....

d) 30 ....

Take a look at the following eight monsters and try to remember what they look like. Then, when you're ready, turn to the next page where some of the monsters will have changed. Can you circle the changes?

Three of the monsters have changed. Can you circle them all?
If you can't find all of the changes, go back to the previous page
and repeat the puzzle until you have spotted them all.

Rearrange the fragments on each line in order to reveal six vegetables.

For example,

RR   CA   OT   can be rearranged to form CARROT.

Now try these:

a) A   PE

b) ON   N   IO

c) TA   PO   TO

d) AG   BB   E   CA

e) MB   CU   CU   ER

f) IF   WER   CA   LO   UL

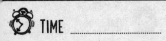

⏰ TIME ....

Can you use your powers of deduction to work out which of the grid squares contain hidden mines in each of these two puzzles? The rules are:

• Any empty grid square can contain a mine, but none of the numbered squares do.

• A number in a square tells you how many mines there are in touching squares, including diagonally touching squares.

Take a look at this example solution to see how it works:

	1	0
☠		1
☠	3	☠

a)

	1		
2		3	1
3		3	1
	3		1

b)

1	2		1
2			2
3			2
	3	2	

How many words of three or more letters can you find hidden in this grid of letters? Start on any letter and then trace a path to touching letters, including diagonally touching letters, to spell out a word. You can't use a letter square more than once in any word. For example, you could start on 'B', move to 'A' and then to 'T' to spell 'BAT'.

There is one word that uses all of the letters.

TARGETS:

Good: 14 words

Excellent: 22 words

Amazing: 30 words

N	I	E
I	A	S
B	R	T

TIME ....

These dragons all look similar, but the group is actually made up of four identical pairs. Can you draw lines to join the dragons into their pairs?

Different countries of the world often use different time zones, meaning that when it's one time in one country it can be a different time in another. Really big countries often have multiple time zones, so, for example, Russia has 11 different time zones.

The time on the west coast of the United States is 8 hours behind the time in the United Kingdom. This means that when it is 11 am in the United Kingdom, it's 3 am in the United States.

Also, the time in France is 1 hour ahead of the time in the United Kingdom, so when it's midday in the United Kingdom then it is 1 pm in France.

Using this information, can you work out the following:

1) When it's 6 pm on the west coast of the United States, what time is it in the United Kingdom?

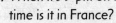

2) When it's 1 am in France, what time is it in the United Kingdom?

....

3) When it's 9 pm on the west coast of the United States, what time is it in France?

....

Can you solve the two Futoshiki puzzles on the opposite page by placing the numbers 1 to 5 once each into every row and column?

You must obey the arrows, which act as 'greater than' and 'less than' signs. The arrows always point from the bigger number to the smaller number of a pair. This means that, for example, you could have '2 > 1' since 2 is greater than 1, but '1 > 2' would be wrong because 1 is not greater in value than 2.

Take a look at this example solution to see how the puzzle works:

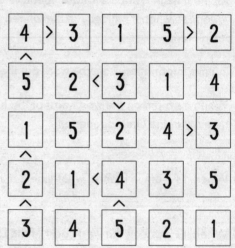

a)

4 <		<		

4 < ☐   ☐ < ☐   ☐

☐ < 3   ☐ < ☐   ☐^

☐   ☐   5   ☐   ☐^

☐˅   ☐   ☐ < 4   ☐

☐   ☐ > ☐ < ☐ < 3

b)

☐   ☐   ☐   ☐   ☐

☐   1   ☐   5   ☐^

☐ > ☐   ☐˅ > ☐   ☐

☐ > 2   ☐ > 3   ☐

☐   ☐ > ☐ > ☐   ☐

Marius, Lucy and Riley are building a model train set, and each is working on a different part. The three parts they are building are a carriage, the train tracks and the train itself. One of them is in the kitchen, one is in the living room and one is in a bedroom.

By reading the following clues, can you complete the empty table to show who is building what, and where?

- Neither Lucy nor Riley are building the train.

- Riley isn't in the living room.

- The carriage isn't being built in the bedroom.

- The train tracks are in the living room.

Person	Part they are building	Where they are building

Can you draw three straight lines in order to divide the area below into five separate regions, so that each region contains exactly one of each type of monster?

Ava, Brooklyn, Charlotte and Daniel all have their birthdays today. By reading the following clues, can you work out which birthday each child is celebrating?

- The oldest child is three times as old as the youngest child.

- The sum of Charlotte and Ava's ages is greater than Brooklyn's age.

- Daniel's age is one year less than the sum of Brooklyn and Charlotte's ages.

- All of the children are less than twelve years old.

- In two years' time, Brooklyn will be twice the age that Charlotte is now.

- The sum of Ava and Brooklyn's ages is equal to Daniel's age.

- At least one child is older than six.

Ava is ....

Brooklyn is ....

Charlotte is ....

Daniel is ....

Can you join all of the dots to form a single loop that visits every dot?

You can only use straight horizontal or vertical lines to join dots, and the loop can't cross or touch itself.

Take a look at this example solution to see how it works:

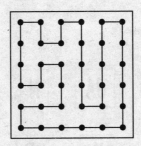

Some parts of the loop have already been drawn in to get you started.

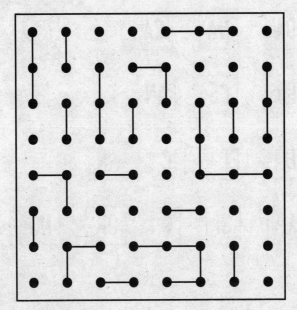

Rearrange the fragments on each line in order to reveal six countries.

For example:

| IN | A | CH |

can be rearranged to form CHINA.

Now try these:

a) | PA | JA | N |

b) | AZ | IL | BR |

c) | DA | NA | CA |

d) | FR | CE | AN |

e) | D | EL | IC | AN |

f) | AP | SI | E | OR | NG |

Can you solve these brain chains in your head, without writing down any numbers until the final answer?

Start with the value at the top of each puzzle, then follow each arrow in turn and do what the mathematical instructions say until you reach the 'RESULT' box. Write the final value you have in that box.

For example in the first puzzle you would start with 39, then divide by 3, then add 30, and so on until you reach the bottom.

a)

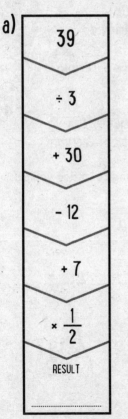

39

÷ 3

+ 30

− 12

+ 7

× $\frac{1}{2}$

RESULT

....

b)

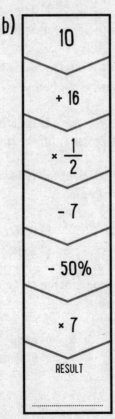

10

+ 16

× $\frac{1}{2}$

− 7

− 50%

× 7

RESULT

....

c)

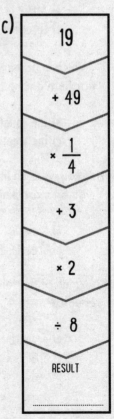

19

+ 49

× $\frac{1}{4}$

+ 3

× 2

÷ 8

RESULT

....

It's quiz time! See how many of the following multiple-choice questions you can answer.

1) Berlin is the capital of which European country?

      a) Belgium   b) France
      c) Germany   d) Norway

2) On which continent would you find Brazil?

      a) Africa   b) Asia
      c) Europe   d) South America

3) Which imaginary line is used to divide the earth into northern and southern hemispheres?

      a) The equator   b) The prime meridian
      c) The tropic of Cancer   d) The tropic of Capricorn

4) If you were an Inuit, which of the following countries would you be most likely to live in:

      a) Gambia   b) Greece
      c) Greenland   d) Guyana

5) Which of the following is not the name of an African country?

      a) Argentina   b) Benin
      c) Chad   d) Djibouti

Can you draw along some of the dashed lines to divide this shape up into four identical pieces, with no unused parts left over?

Each of the four pieces must be identical, although they can be rotated relative to one another.

Take a look at this example solution to see how it works:

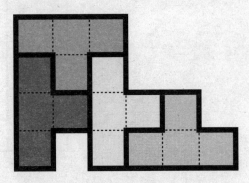

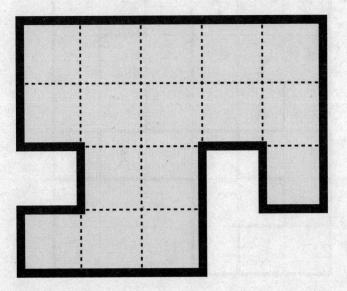

Can you complete these grids so that every row, column and bold-lined region contains each letter from A to F once each?

This example solution helps show you how it works:

F	C	D	E	B	A
E	B	A	F	C	D
C	A	E	B	D	F
A	D	B	C	F	E
B	E	F	D	A	C
D	F	C	A	E	B

a)

E		C			
F					
	A				
				A	
					D
			C		E

b)

	B	A			
D			C		
		F			D
			A	B	

Can you solve this crossword in which all the clues are written within the grid?

Violent windstorm	▼	Visible parts of a fire	▼	The blackened remains of a fire	▼	Moving image screen	▼	Device for taking pictures
Region; the space occupied by something		Have a meal, for example		Remain in the same place ▶		▼		
▶		▼		Folded and sewn edge of cloth ▶				Fetch; obtain
Something by which a person is called				Part of the body containing your knee ▶				▼
Had some food				At this place ▶				
Common family pet		Practical joke		Make a serious promise	Large container for liquids ▶			
▶		▼		Narrow runner for use on snow ▶	▼		And this thing too	Happy
Quarrel; disagree	A long, thin stick, such as one used for fishing		Utilize		Droop to a lower level ▶		▼	▼
▶	▼		▼		Sick; not well			
Small, poisonous snake		Triangular Indian snack ▶						
▶					Head movement used to signal 'yes' ▶			

Can you find a path all the way through this maze? Enter at the top and exit at the bottom, as shown. It's trickier than it looks, since the maze also includes bridges. On each bridge you can either travel over the bridge or travel under it. (You can't turn right or left while crossing over or going under a bridge.)

Part of the path is drawn in, to show you how it works:

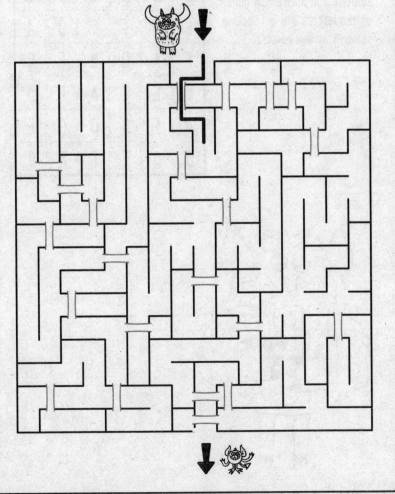

Can you place a letter from A to F into every empty square, so that no letter repeats in any row or column? Identical letters can't be in touching squares — not even diagonally.

Take a look at this example solution and notice how none of the letters are in touching squares at any point:

C	D	A	E	B	F
E	B	F	C	D	A
F	A	D	B	E	C
B	E	C	A	F	D
A	F	B	D	C	E
D	C	E	F	A	B

a)

E					D
		D	E		
	A			F	
	E			D	
		C	B		
C					B

b)

D		C	B		E
E					F
A					D
F		B	E		A

Can you find all of the listed animals in the grid? They can be written either forwards or backwards and can run in any direction, including diagonally.

There's just one problem — the grid isn't yet complete. While solving it, you'll need to fill in the letters that should go in the central 5×5 area, with one letter per square. There's only one way to do this and fit in all 21 animals.

BEAR	HAMSTER	RABBIT
CAMEL	HORSE	SHEEP
ELEPHANT	IGUANA	TIGER
FROG	LION	TORTOISE
GIRAFFE	LLAMA	TURTLE
GORILLA	MONKEY	WOLF
GUINEA PIG	MOUSE	ZEBRA

E	G	L	U	G	H	O	R	S	E	I
Z	L	O	E	S	I	O	T	R	O	T
Y	E	I	R	M	S	R	R	R	W	M
E	A	B						I	O	O
K	I	R						F	L	U
N	A	R						E	F	S
O	T	U						T	P	E
M	G	G						I	U	G
I	R	E	T	S	M	A	H	G	A	E
E	L	E	P	H	A	N	T	E	H	A
A	T	I	B	B	A	R	F	R	O	G

Imagine sliding these columns of letters up and down so that different words become visible through horizontal window. The word 'LANES' is made already, but if you were to slide the first column up one letter then you could make 'MANES', and so on.

By sliding columns, can you find:

1) **Three words beginning with 'L':**

....

2) **Three fruit:** ....

3) **A month:** ....

4) **Three words with 'T' as their middle letter:**

....

5) **Three words that end with an 'E':**

....

You can use words more than once if you wish, but if you fancy a trickier challenge then try to answer all five questions without repeating any words.

Can you complete this crossword grid by adding each letter from A to Z once each, so every horizontal and vertical sequence of letters spells out a word? Use the letters outside the grid to keep track of which ones you've already placed.

A	I		I				C					N
B	D	A	N		E		A		A	R	D	O
C				S				S				P
D	A		U	A	T		C			E	E	Q
E	A		U	A	T		C			E	E	R
F			R				E				N	S
G		U	Y	E			L	I			T	T
H	A			E				R				U
I	A											V
J	L	A	B		S	E	A	O				W
K		A		U		R				U	X
L	E	C	E	L			I	N	U	S	Y
M	T						D			K	Z

All
of the
ANSWERS

AMAZING BRAIN GAME 1

The correct jigsaw piece is c.

AMAZING BRAIN GAME 2

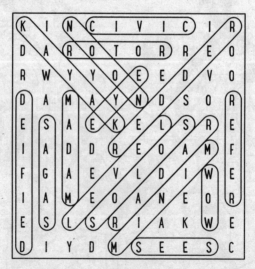

AMAZING BRAIN GAME 3

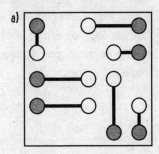

a)

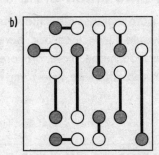

b)

AMAZING BRAIN GAME 4

1) b – at each stage the polygon has one less side, becomes smaller, and alternates between black and white

2) c – at each stage the circle moves clockwise around the image, and another line is added to the square being drawn in the middle of the picture

AMAZING BRAIN GAME 5

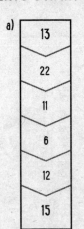

a)
13
22
11
6
12
15

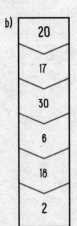

b)
20
17
30
6
18
2

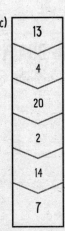

c)
13
4
20
2
14
7

AMAZING BRAIN GAME 6

The word that uses all of the letters is 'problem'. Other words that you could find include: bop, bore, lob, lobe, lop, lope, lore, mob, mole, mop, mope, more, orb, ore, poem, pole, pore, pro, probe, prom, rob, robe, roe, role, romp and rope.

AMAZING BRAIN GAME 7

1) (Example) I am proud to OWN lots of trophies that I have WON.
2) We keep the largest cooking POT on the TOP shelf.
3) The LAST thing to add to the recipe is some SALT.
4) On the way to school, I STOP to POST my letters in the box.
5) I accidentally knocked my arm just BELOW the ELBOW.
6) It's easier to LISTEN when everyone else is SILENT.
7) At the store, they gave me a TASTER of some sweet TREATS.
8) These PLATES feature a design made up of flower PETALS.

AMAZING BRAIN GAME 8

Picture b is the odd-one-out.

AMAZING BRAIN GAME 9

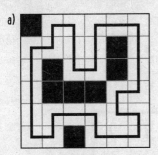

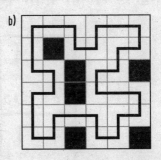

AMAZING BRAIN GAME 10

$11 = 1 + 2 + 8$
$16 = 4 + 5 + 7$
$26 = 9 + 10 + 7$

AMAZING BRAIN GAME 11

There are 13 circles
in total.

AMAZING BRAIN GAME 12

a)

1	4	2	3
2	3	1	4
4	1	3	2
3	2	4	1

b)

1	4	3	2
2	3	4	1
4	1	2	3
3	2	1	4

c)

2	4	3	1
1	3	4	2
3	1	2	4
4	2	1	3

AMAZING BRAIN GAME 13

Possible words include: BEG, BIB, BIG, BIN, BUG, BUN, RIB, RIG, RUB, RUG, RUN (given as the example), TEN, TIN, TUB, TUG, WEB, WIG and WIN.

AMAZING BRAIN GAME 14

AMAZING BRAIN GAME 15

a)

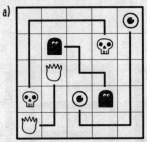

b)

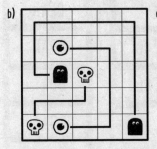

c)

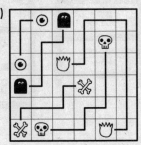

AMAZING BRAIN GAME 16

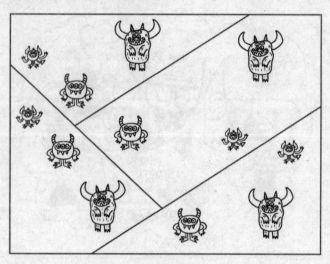

AMAZING BRAIN GAME 17

Some possible solutions are:

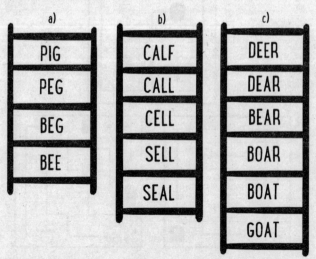

AMAZING BRAIN GAME 18

a)

41

21	20

11	10	10

b)

34

19	15

13	6	9

c)

32

19	13

12	7	6

8	4	3	3

AMAZING BRAIN GAME 19

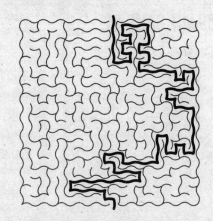

AMAZING BRAIN GAME 20

AMAZING BRAIN GAME 21

1 ⬇	9 ➡	10 ⬇	8 ⬅
5 ➡	4 ⬅	11 ⬇	6 ⬇
2 ➡	3 ⬆	12 ⬇	7 ⬆
14 ➡	15 ➡	13 ⬅	16

AMAZING BRAIN GAME 22

They are all numbers:

1) TWO
2) SEVEN
3) NINE
4) TWELVE
5) TWENTY
6) ELEVEN

AMAZING BRAIN GAME 23

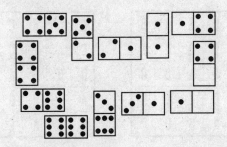

AMAZING BRAIN GAME 24

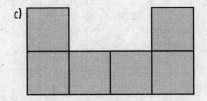

AMAZING BRAIN GAME 25

The total is 29.

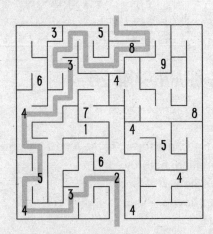

AMAZING BRAIN GAME 26

a)

D	C	E	A	B
A	B	D	C	E
C	E	A	B	D
B	D	C	E	A
E	A	B	D	C

b)

E	D	B	C	A
C	A	E	D	B
D	B	C	A	E
A	E	D	B	C
B	C	A	E	D

AMAZING BRAIN GAME 27

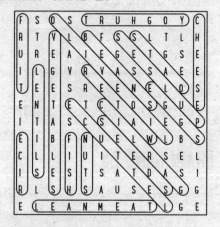

AMAZING BRAIN GAME 28

a) 36 eyes

b) 14 monsters

c) 3 monsters – 2 are facing to the left of the page, and 1 has its eye pointing that way

d) 2 monsters have five limbs

e) 3 monsters have six limbs

f) 8 monsters

AMAZING BRAIN GAME 29

a) 48 – add 7 at each step
b) 43 – subtract 12 at each step
c) 4 – divide by 2 at each step
d) 789 – add 111 at each step
e) 243 – multiply by 3 at each step

AMAZING BRAIN GAME 30

AMAZING BRAIN GAME 31

a)

4	5	6	7
3	10	9	8
2	11	14	15
1	12	13	16

b)

1	8	9	16
2	7	10	15
3	6	11	14
4	5	12	13

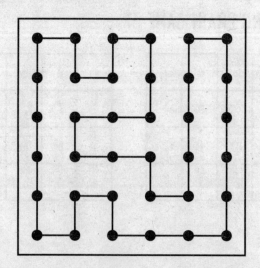

AMAZING BRAIN GAME 32

The word that uses all of the letters is 'mysteries'. Other words that can be found include: ire, reset, resets, rest, rye, see, seer, seers, sees, series, set, sets, steer, steers, tee, tees, term, terms, terse, tree, trees, tries, try, yes and yeses.

AMAZING BRAIN GAME 33

a) 10: Burst 3, 8 and 9 to leave 4 + 6
b) 16: Burst 6 and 8 to leave 3 + 4 + 9
c) 26: Burst 4 to leave 3 + 6 + 8 + 9.

AMAZING BRAIN GAME 34

AMAZING BRAIN GAME 35

AMAZING BRAIN GAME 36

24 cubes: 4 cubes on the top layer, 7 cubes on the middle layer and 13 cubes on the bottom layer

AMAZING BRAIN GAME 37

1b, 2d, 3d, 4c, 5b

AMAZING BRAIN GAME 38

a)

4	3	1	2
2	1 < 3	4
1	4	2 < 3
3	2	4 > 1

b)

4	2	1	3
3	1	2	4
1	4	3 > 2
2	3	4	1

AMAZING BRAIN GAME 39

P	R	E	S	E	N	T		S	E	A
O		M		N		R		E		R
L	I	P		G	L	I	T	T	E	R
I		E		I		O				A
T	H	R	O	N	E		S	C	A	N
I		O		E		G		O		G
C	O	R	E		C	A	S	T	L	E
I				L		T		T		M
A	T	H	L	E	T	E		A	W	E
N		U		N		A		G		N
S	U	M		S	T	U	D	E	N	T

AMAZING BRAIN GAME 40

T	A	S	T	E		
I		C		V	E	T
S	N	O	R	E		I
S		O		N		C
U		T	R	I	C	K
E	Y	E		N		E
		R	I	G	H	T

AMAZING BRAIN GAME 41

a)

2	☠	1
☠	3	
1		☠

b)

☠	☠	1
☠	4	2
1		☠

AMAZING BRAIN GAME 42

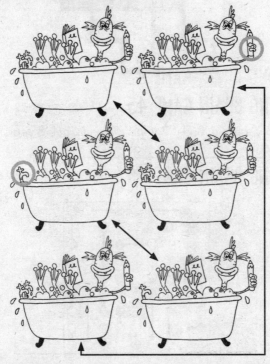

AMAZING BRAIN GAME 43

1) EAR
2) CARE
3) CRANE
4) NECTAR
5) CERTAIN
6) CLARINET

AMAZING BRAIN GAME 44

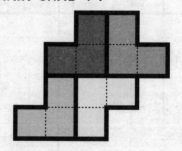

AMAZING BRAIN GAME 45

Amy is 5 years old, Bud is 7 years old and Cat is 8 years old.

AMAZING BRAIN GAME 46

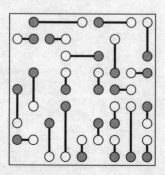

AMAZING BRAIN GAME 47

The missing items are the scissors, the apple and the book.

AMAZING BRAIN GAME 48

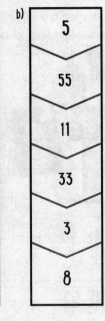

a)

17
30
29
33
11
22

b)

5
55
11
33
3
8

c)

13
78
67
73
65
72

AMAZING BRAIN GAME 49

Person	Part they are playing	Hat they are wearing
Bobbie	Hippolyta	Orange
Heather	Hermia	Green
Nadia	Helena	Purple

AMAZING BRAIN GAME 50

1) c – at each stage, the shaded square moves clockwise
   around the image, and an additional diagonal line is
   added (also, each diagonal-lined shape starts opposite
   the shaded square in each image)

2) b – at each stage, the polygon has one more side;
   and there are always two straight lines outside the polygon

AMAZING BRAIN GAME 51

AMAZING BRAIN GAME 52

a)

5	1	6	2	4	3
4	2	3	5	1	6
3	6	1	4	2	5
2	3	4	6	5	1
6	4	5	1	3	2
1	5	2	3	6	4

b)

5	4	2	1	6	3
6	2	4	3	1	5
1	3	6	5	2	4
4	6	3	2	5	1
3	5	1	6	4	2
2	1	5	4	3	6

AMAZING BRAIN GAME 53

1) 7c, since the five 10c coins have a total value of 50c
2) Four coins: 50c + 20c + 10c + 5c
3) Something costing 88c, since 1c + 2c + 5c + 10c + 20c + 50c = 88c
4) Seven coins: 1c + 2c + 2c + 5c + 10c + 10c + 20c

AMAZING BRAIN GAME 54

e)

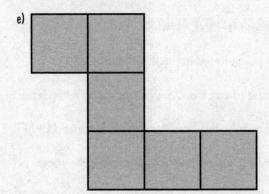

AMAZING BRAIN GAME 55

Some possible solutions are:

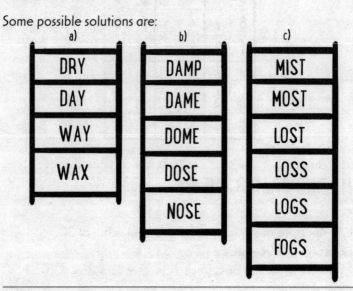

a)

DRY
DAY
WAY
WAX

b)

DAMP
DAME
DOME
DOSE
NOSE

c)

MIST
MOST
LOST
LOSS
LOGS
FOGS

AMAZING BRAIN GAME 56

1) (Example) I rubbed some GEL on my sore LEG.

2) The OWL flew very LOW over the field.

3) Sometimes I feel WEAK when I first WAKE up.

4) The magician found her WAND at DAWN.

5) I managed to catch and SAVE the VASE when it fell over.

6) In the dim light, the PEARL on the ring looked PALER.

7) The CAPED superhero PACED around the room.

8) When the ground QUAKES, I hear my pet mouse SQUEAK.

AMAZING BRAIN GAME 57

```
      S P A G H E T T I
    E   O   L     A   E     A
    V I D E O   S T A N D
    E       V     Y   C     V
    R O B B E R   S H O E
    Y   L   S     S   E     N
    B O O K   P A R R O T
    O   S   C     F       U
    D I S C O   A F T E R
    Y   O   L     R   O     E
      I M P A T I E N T
```

AMAZING BRAIN GAME 58

```
    F L E A   T I C K
  P   L   P E W   H     V
  A M A Z E   E V A D E
  R   M   X   N   R     G
  T R A P   S T A T U E
  R       T   Y       T
  I N S E R T   T U N A B
  D   T   O   J   S   B
  G R O U P   E Q U A L
  E   N   H O E   A   E
    V E R Y   R U L E
```

AMAZING BRAIN GAME 59

AMAZING BRAIN GAME 60

19 = 2 + 5 + 12
28 = 9 + 8 + 11
33 = 9 + 13 + 11

AMAZING BRAIN GAME 61

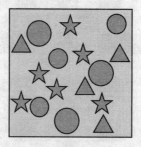

a) 6 stars   b) 6 circles   c) 4 triangles

AMAZING BRAIN GAME 62

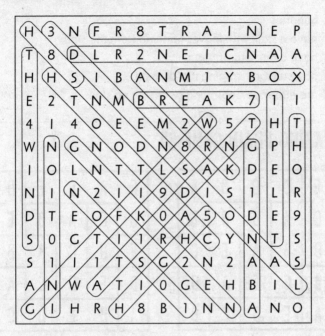

AMAZING BRAIN GAME 63

One word that uses all of the letters is 'monster', and you might also have found 'mentors', too. Other words that you could find include: mentor, met, metro, metros, most, mote, motes, nest, net, nets, not, note, notes, onset, rent, rents, rest, rot, rote, rots, sent, set, smote, snort, sort, stem, stern, stone, store, storm, ten, tenor, tenors, tens, tensor, term, terms, tern, terns, toe, toes, tom, tome, tomes, toms, ton, tone, toner, tones, tons, tor, tore, torn and tors.

AMAZING BRAIN GAME 64

1) 3 bananas
2) 5 have a stalk with leaves hanging from the stalk
3) 7 have a bite out of them
4) 7 have a worm coming out of them
5) 4 are either an apple or a pear with no stalk

AMAZING BRAIN GAME 65

a)

E	D	C	B	A
C	A	B	D	E
D	B	A	E	C
B	C	E	A	D
A	E	D	C	B

b)

C	A	B	E	D
D	C	A	B	E
E	D	C	A	B
B	E	D	C	A
A	B	E	D	C

AMAZING BRAIN GAME 66

1 →	4 ↙	9 ↙	2 ↓
5 ↓	10 ↓	14 ↙	8 ↖
6 →	12 ↘	7 ↗	3 ↖
15 →	11 ↑	13 ↑	16

AMAZING BRAIN GAME 67

32 cubes: 3 cubes on the top layer, 5 cubes on the second layer down, 10 cubes on the third layer down, and 14 cubes on the bottom layer

AMAZING BRAIN GAME 68

AMAZING BRAIN GAME 69

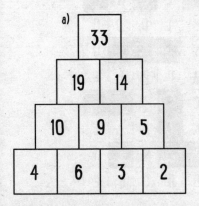

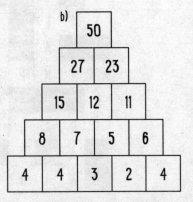

AMAZING BRAIN GAME 70

Person	Race they won a medal in	Medal they won
Carrie	100m sprint	Bronze
Mohammed	Long jump	Silver
Tallulah	400m sprint	Gold

AMAZING BRAIN GAME 71

1) ASK
2) TASK
3) STAKE
4) BASKET
5) SETBACK
6) BRACKETS

AMAZING BRAIN GAME 72

A	C	C	I	D	E	N	T	
R		L			E		W	
T	I	E		B	L	O	O	D
		A		L				U
P	I	N	E	A	P	P	L	E
O				C		I		
T	R	A	C	K		A	L	L
	A		A			N		I
	W	A	R	D	R	O	B	E

AMAZING BRAIN GAME 73

Monster d.

AMAZING BRAIN GAME 74

25	14	13	12	11
24	15	2	3	10
23	16	1	4	9
22	17	18	5	8
21	20	19	6	7

AMAZING BRAIN GAME 75

AMAZING BRAIN GAME 76

a)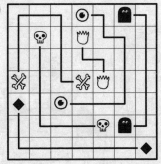

b)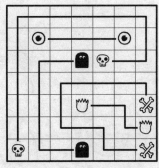

AMAZING BRAIN GAME 77

They are all fruit:

1) LIME (shift each letter back one place)
2) MELON (shift each letter forward one place)
3) APPLE (shift each letter back one place)
4) GRAPE (shift each letter back one place)
5) CHERRY (shift each letter forward one place)
6) PINEAPPLE (shift each letter back one place)

AMAZING BRAIN GAME 78

There are 43 rectangles to be found.

AMAZING BRAIN GAME 79

15: Burst 4, 5, 9 and 12 to leave 7 + 8
18: Burst 7, 8 and 12 to leave 4 + 5 + 9
23: Burst 5, 8 and 9 to leave 4 + 7 + 12
30: Burst 7 and 8 to leave 4 + 5 + 9 + 12

AMAZING BRAIN GAME 80

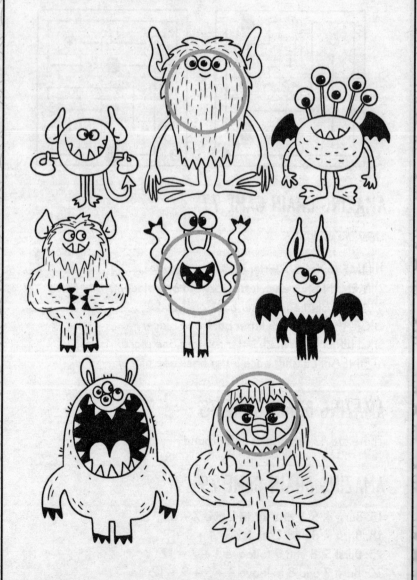

AMAZING BRAIN GAME 81

a) PEA
b) ONION
c) POTATO
d) CABBAGE
e) CUCUMBER
f) CAULIFLOWER

AMAZING BRAIN GAME 82

a)

	1		☠
2	☠	3	1
3	☠	3	1
☠	3	☠	1

b)

1	2		1
2	☠	☠	2
3	☠	☠	2
☠	3	2	

AMAZING BRAIN GAME 83

The word that uses all of the letters is 'brainiest'. Other words that can be found include: air, airs, anise, art, arts, ban, bar, bars, base, basin, bat, bats, bias, bin, bra, brain, braise, bran, bras, brat, brats, briniest, ear, ears, east, eat, eats, nab, nib, rain, rainiest, raise, ran, rat, rats, rib, sari, sat, sea, sear, seat, sin, stain, stair, star, strain, tab, tan, tar, tars, train and tsar.

AMAZING BRAIN GAME 84

AMAZING BRAIN GAME 85

1) 2 am

2) 12 am (midnight)

3) 6 am

AMAZING BRAIN GAME 86

a)

4 <	5	2 <	3	1
1 <	3	4 <	5	2
3	2	5	1	4
2	1	3 <	4	5
5	4 >	1 <	2 <	3

b)

3	5	1	4	2
2	1	4	5	3
5 >	3	2 >	1	4
4 >	2	5 >	3	1
1	4 >	3 >	2	5

AMAZING BRAIN GAME 87

Person	Part they are building	Where they are building
Marius	Train	Bedroom
Riley	Carriage	Kitchen
Lucy	Train tracks	Living room

AMAZING BRAIN GAME 88

AMAZING BRAIN GAME 89

Ava is 3 years old, Brooklyn is 6 years old, Charlotte is 4 years old and Daniel is 9 years old.

AMAZING BRAIN GAME 90

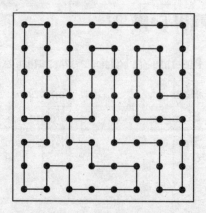

AMAZING BRAIN GAME 91

a) JAPAN

b) BRAZIL

c) CANADA

d) FRANCE

e) ICELAND

f) SINGAPORE

AMAZING BRAIN GAME 92

a)
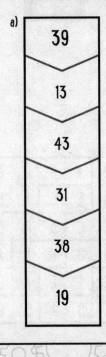
39
13
43
31
38
19

b)
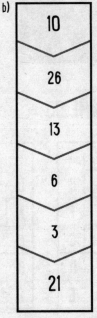
10
26
13
6
3
21

c)
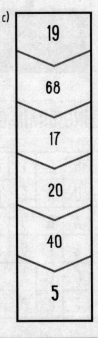
19
68
17
20
40
5

AMAZING BRAIN GAME 93

1c, 2d, 3a, 4c, 5a (Argentina is in South America)

AMAZING BRAIN GAME 94

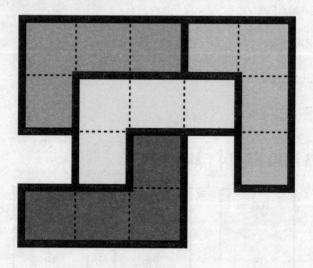

AMAZING BRAIN GAME 95

a)

E	B	C	F	D	A
F	D	A	E	C	B
C	A	B	D	E	F
D	E	F	B	A	C
B	C	E	A	F	D
A	F	D	C	B	E

b)

F	B	A	D	C	E
D	A	E	C	F	B
A	E	C	B	D	F
C	D	B	F	E	A
B	C	F	E	A	D
E	F	D	A	B	C

AMAZING BRAIN GAME 96

	T		F		A		C	
	O		L		S	T	A	Y
A	R	E	A		H	E	M	
	N	A	M	E		L	E	G
	A	T	E		H	E	R	E
	D		S			V	A	T
D	O	G		S	K	I		
		A		W		S	A	G
A	R	G	U	E		I	L	L
	O		S	A	M	O	S	A
A	D	D	E	R		N	O	D

AMAZING BRAIN GAME 97

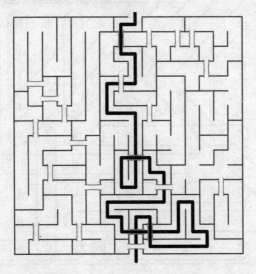

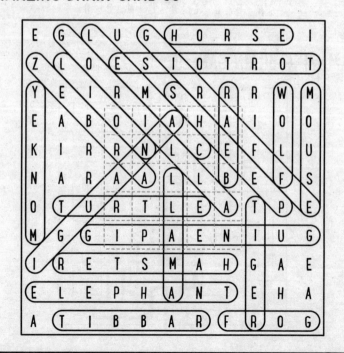

ANSWERS

AMAZING BRAIN GAME 98

a)

E	B	A	F	C	D
F	C	D	E	B	A
D	A	B	C	F	E
B	E	F	A	D	C
A	D	C	B	E	F
C	F	E	D	A	B

b)

D	F	C	B	A	E
B	A	E	F	D	C
E	C	D	A	B	F
A	B	F	C	E	D
C	E	A	D	F	B
F	D	B	E	C	A

AMAZING BRAIN GAME 99

AMAZING BRAIN GAME 100

1) Words beginning with 'L' include LANCE, LANES, LARCH, LARGE, LARGO, LATCH, LEACH, LEAPS, LONGS and LORES.
2) Fruit: GRAPE, MANGO, PEACH
3) A month: MARCH
4) Words with 'T' as their middle letter include GATES, LATCH, MATCH, MATES, PATCH and PATES.
5) Words that end with 'E' include GRACE, GRAPE, PEACE, LANCE, MANGE, PENCE, GORGE, LARGE, MARGE and MERGE.

AMAZING BRAIN GAME 101

I		I		Z		C	P	A
D	A	N	C	E		A	W	A	R	D
E		J		S		A	S		V
A	Q	U	A	T	I	C		S	E	E	N
		R		T		E			E
B	U	Y	E	R			L	I	G	H	T
A				E			R	
L	A	B		S	E	A	F	O	O	D
L		A		U		R		U		U
E	X	C	E	L		M	I	N	U	S
T		K		T		Y		D		K

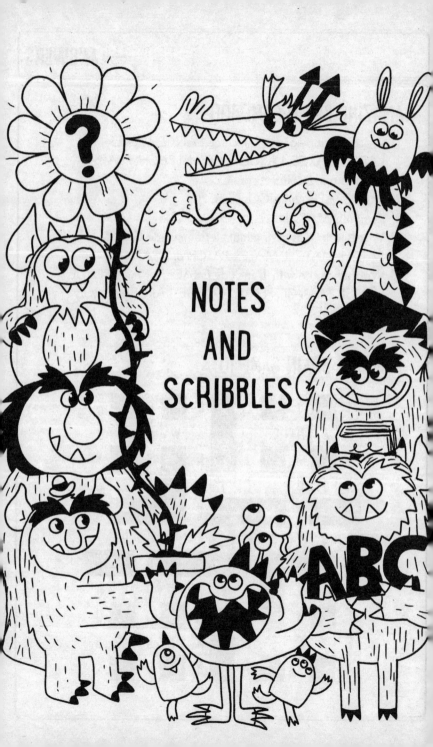

NOTES
AND
SCRIBBLES

NOTES AND SCRIBBLES →

NOTES AND SCRIBBLES

NOTES AND SCRIBBLES →